ParentSmart Books™

Your Baby and Child's

Emotional and Social Development

D0921913

Penny A. Shore

with

 The International Advisory Council on Parenting

Penelope Leach, Ph.D.

William Sears, M.D.

Martha Sears, R.N.

Otto Weininger, Ph.D.

Canadian Cataloguing in Publication Data

Shore, Penny A.
Your baby & child's emotional & social development

ISBN 1-896833-15-2

Includes index. 1. Child development. 2. Parenting. 3. Child rearing. I.International Advisory Council on
Parenting. II. Title. III. Title: Your baby and child's emotional and social development. IV. Series:
Shore, Penny A. Parent**Smart** Books.

HQ774.S52 2002   649'.1   C2001-901958-0

Published by The Parent Kit Corporation
2 Bloor Street West, Suite 1720
Toronto, Ontario M4W 3E2

Printed in Canada, by St. Joseph Printing Ltd.
First printing November 2001

1 2 3 4 5   05 04 03 02 01

ParentSmart Books
introduction to the series

Parenting has been my passion ever since the day my first child was born. This was, without doubt, an exhilarating and exciting event. However, it didn't take long to realize that with the birth of our child, we were taking on one of the most important jobs in life – and one for which we hadn't taken a training course. Furthermore, the baby didn't come with an instruction manual!

Now, my children have grown into happy, successful young adults and although my job is educational publishing, I have always considered parenting to be my most satisfying career. About four years ago, it occurred to me that I could combine my passion for parenting with my publishing experience. The idea was to produce a series of books designed to give new parents the very help and guidance I was looking for as a new parent. To develop the content, four of the world's leading parenting authorities were recruited to join me in establishing The International Advisory Council on Parenting. The members are; Penelope Leach, Ph.D., Otto Weininger, Ph.D., William Sears, M.D. and Martha Sears, R.N. The result of our combined efforts is the Parent**Smart** book series.

Despite the daily challenges faced by parents, there is probably no job in the world that matches parenting in terms of personal fulfillment and truly wonderful fringe benefits.

Parents who are properly prepared with the right tools and skills will have less stress and are likely to be more effective. That's why each book in the Parent**Smart** book series deals with one particular aspect of parenting. Taken together, the first six books in the series combine to provide a virtual "Parenting 101" course.

These books are unique in many ways. They provide you with a combination of expert information, interactive exercises and journals where you can record important information about your child. By having the full series available in your home, you will have easy access to the knowledge and support you will need to confidently handle most parenting situations.

There is another feature of the Parent**Smart** series that is very special. The experts don't necessarily agree on all parenting issues, and this can be confusing to parents who want their child to benefit from the best advice. We resolved this by having all members of The International Advisory Council on Parenting approve and come to consensus on the content.

A complete list of the other titles in this series, and a description of their contents, can be found at the back of this book. Parent**Smart** books are also a good refresher and primer for new grandparents, child caretakers and others in your extended family who will interact with your child.

Try to complete the questionnaires and exercises when you can. This will help you and your parenting partner to have a basis for communicating on the important issues and to be a better parenting team. The journals will provide records that you can enjoy and share with your children when they are older. "Tips and Techniques" are highlighted in the book to help you make immediate use of your new skills in every day situations.

I hope this book will raise your awareness about important parenting issues and give you the confidence to be a more effective and nurturing parent. Nothing can match the pleasure and happiness of seeing your children grow into fulfilled adults who are getting the best from their lives and whose friendship you cherish.

It has now been well-established that investing in your child's first three years will pay dividends in determining his or her future development. So, good luck with this stage and may your parenting adventure be one of the most rewarding experiences of your lifetime.

Penny Shore

dedication

To Joan, Eric, Jay and Amanda —
from whom I continue to learn.

Your Baby and Child's
Emotional and Social Development

Table of Contents

Give a little love to your child and you get a great deal back.

John Ruskin

the chance
of a lifetime

introduction

NOTES

Emotional growth is a never ending process. It can't be charted on a graph or measured easily, and it isn't as predictable as physical growth. Physical development takes place in a certain order, each stage depending on the stage before. Crawling usually comes before walking, and walking comes before running. Emotional development also takes place step by step, but it is a unique meandering journey with challenging ups and downs. It depends on a complex blend of relationships, experiences, personalities, temperaments and other factors. Your baby will develop from a bundle of sensations, to an individual with a sense of herself, to an independent person. As she learns to take baby steps with her legs, she depends on you to give her a hand to cling to and plenty of encouragement. While she takes tiny

emotional steps that you can't see, she also needs your encouragement and guidance. Humans are social beings who need each other. No baby can do it alone.

The building blocks of physical health are good nutrition, proper medical care and regular exercise. Your baby's emotional building blocks are made out of the relationships that she shares with you and her important caregivers. First she learns to love, trust and rely on you by holding on to you in any way she can. Then she learns to carry that sense of trust with her by remembering you when the two of you are apart. Finally, she develops her own independence by learning how to trust others. Everything she needs to know about human relationships she learns through her passionate attachment to you and yours to her.

Your baby needs attentive, responsive, sensitive care to thrive physically and develop emotionally. In the first two years of life, physical care and emotional growth work hand in glove. Watching her grow and develop physically is exciting. Nurturing her emotions with love is mutually enriching. There is nothing more gratifying than a deep, trusting bond between you and your child.

This book gives you the basic information you need to know about how a baby develops emotionally, and describes the skills and techniques that help to create a strong, healthy relationship. While some emotions are innate, feelings develop within relationships, through interaction, shared experiences, communication and even a little conflict. Your baby's first relationships with her caregivers teach her basic emotional skills and responses, and set the path for later emotional development.

When she feels loved and cared for, your baby develops a sense of security that allows her to explore her world and develop at her own pace. She needs that to meet the challenges of growing, developing and becoming independent.

Note: *Alternating between feminine and masculine gender in text can be confusing. So, for the sake of clarity, this book will use "she." The information applies equally to boys and girls, unless otherwise specified.*

the parent partnership

Parents and caregivers are the senior partners, and the baby begins as the junior partner. As your baby develops, the partnership will change, but if you start with an attentive, responsive approach, that will make for an effective agreement.

The first step in parenting by partnership is recognizing that your baby is an individual with her own personality, her own needs, and her own abilities. To be her partner, you must find out who your baby is by letting her tell you, rather than by you telling her. You can do this by observing her carefully and letting her show you her own rhythms, appetites and expressions.

Think of your baby as a charming new guest. Would you tell any other guest how many hours she should sleep and when she should eat? You would encourage her to tell you, and you would listen to what she says. That way you can meet your guest's unique and personal needs, and you can learn about

> It is one of the most beautiful compensations of this life that no man can sincerely try to help another without helping himself.
>
> **RALPH WALDO EMERSON**

your baby's particular needs the same way. She will cry when she's hungry, close her eyes when she's sleepy, fuss when she feels uncomfortable and do an amazing job at introducing herself to you. Watching your baby carefully, listening to her signals, and engaging in a little trial and error will work most of the time.

In great relationships, the feelings are strong on both sides. You will have a powerful impact on your baby and she will have a major impact on you. Be prepared to throw yourself into this relationship body and soul, and enjoy the passion.

The intensity of parenthood can be surprising. As you watch your child develop you may experience some unexpected memories. This is a wonderful chance to revisit the best of your past, and if you relax and enjoy it, you almost get a second childhood. You may also re-experience some of the childhood struggles that you had forgotten. Even if this is rather disturbing, it is a very good sign. It means you are emotionally tuned in to your baby. Babies express their feelings spontaneously, without restraint, so that adults can observe them and respond to them.

Pat's six-month-old baby boy, Daniel, was the ever-smiling, jolly baby. She chose to stay home and be his primary caregiver, so they were together most of the time. Because she had no budget for babysitters, she went just about everywhere with him, even to social events where he was the only baby. One evening, Pat, her husband Richard, and Daniel were at a dinner party. Daniel was on the carpet with a couple of his favorite traveling toys and the adults were sitting around comfortably, having a glass of wine. Suddenly, Daniel began to cry a dissatisfied, fretful sort of cry that was persistent but not too intense. Pat was surprised, and commented that Daniel had been fed and changed and seemed quite contented until that moment. Then she saw Daniel looking at her glass, and then turning his head to look at Richard's glass. As if a light bulb had gone off, she laughed and reached into her baby bag to hand Daniel a bottle of water, which he took with a big smile. "He saw all of us drinking," said Pat, "and wanted to be included."

This is a partnership of many parts. The basic partnership is between the baby, her parents and her primary caregivers, but it generates many new partnerships. Babysitters, siblings, grandparents, friends, doctors, teachers and other community members will all take their parts. You cannot do it entirely on your own. Co-parenting will change your relationship to each other, as well. All couples make their own choices about how child care is shared. Today, many dads have a very active, hands-on role from the start.

Single parents, working parents and parents who share custody, all need to find ways to convey their parenting approach to the other people involved with their children. Information in this book can be shared with your other parenting partners.

POINTS TO REMEMBER

- Emotional development depends on a complex blend of relationships, experiences, personalities, temperaments and other factors.
- Your baby will develop a base with you for love and trust. This base sets the stage for her future emotional development.
- Listen to your baby and watch for signals. She will let you know what she is feeling and what she wants.

your baby's emotional development

emotions and the brain

While basic brain development takes place in utero, more has to happen after birth once the baby's head has made it through the birth canal. When your baby is born, her brain is already the central operating system for many things, including keeping the lungs breathing, the heart beating and other physical functions. Other cerebral abilities exist in a primitive state which will develop further through stimulation. For example, your baby has the ability to use her eyes at birth, but her visual acuity develops through stimulation of the brain cells that lead from the eye to the brain. Parents can provide a mobile over the crib to provide that stimulation.

The cells of the brain, which are called neurons, form themselves into increasingly complicated chains after birth through the stimulation they receive throughout infancy and childhood. When stimuli is provided, the neurons respond by organizing into chains. Where the neurons meet, a connection called a synapse forms. These synapses are like the links of a chain, connecting neuron after neuron together into intricate cords and strands that permit complicated brain activity. Information passes along these strands the way electricity passes along a wire.

After birth, your baby's brain continues to develop more synapses in vast numbers. The brain is acutely responsive to stimulation and can develop an impressive number of abilities, depending on what it is asked to do. This is why infancy and childhood are the most important phases of life for learning. Once the chains of neurons are in place and used a certain way over and over, they stay in that formation. They remain as networks which enable the baby to carry out actions that are required by certain stimulations.

The degree to which I can create relationships which facilitate the growth of others as separate persons is a measure of the growth I have achieved in myself.

CARL ROGERS

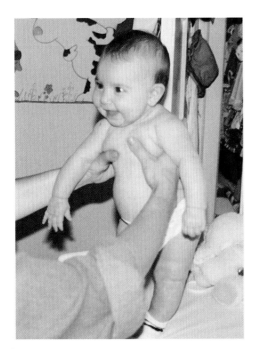

But in order for those brain networks to start being used properly, they need to be organized so that information can be passed from cell to cell in an orderly fashion. Feeding, holding, changing, bathing, rocking, looking at, singing to and talking to your newborn are all ways of providing stimulation. High-quality stimulation creates a richer brain, just as high-quality nutrition creates a healthier body. Your baby's brain is ready and waiting to receive that stimulation and use it to make the brain develop more. All the stimulation you give her will strengthen her total development.

But how do you know which stimulus to provide, when, in what quantity, and in what way? Amazingly enough, from the moment of birth, your baby tells you what she needs. A newborn has reflexes to get her message across – rooting for milk; startling if you're not holding her securely enough; crying for other comforts; and sleeping when she needs a break from stimulation. A newborn needs her creature comforts and lets you know it, but she is really doing something more at the same time. In a way, she is asking you for input from the outside world so she can organize it in her head. She's asking you to feed her brain.

Although we talk about feelings coming from our hearts, we really feel emotions in our brain, which has a special part called the limbic system that controls emotion. This part of the brain fits like a ring over the top of the brainstem. Above that is another part of the brain called the neocortex, which controls rational thought. In the human brain, neurons connect the limbic system to the neocortex so that emotional information gets through to the rational part, and rational information penetrates the emotional part, as well. This allows us to combine thoughts and feelings in a complex way.

Your baby's limbic system has to get organized to have feelings, just as her neocortex has to get organized to have thoughts. For example, a baby begins to recognize her caregiver's sound and smell within hours of birth, and stores this sense data in her limbic system. As her sight becomes more developed, information travels between the retina and the brain so that visual information is added to the sound and smell data. Eventually, the sight, sound and smell data that your baby has stored in her limbic system produces an emotional expression of recognition and pleasure called a smile.

Your normal, spontaneous reaction is to smile back. This actually teaches her that smiles communicate what she feels. You make her happiness real by giving back the smile she gave you. Then her happiness doubles. She can feel her own happiness and see your happiness, and this teaches her that feelings can be shared.

This all happens so spontaneously that it doesn't seem like learning, but it is. Your baby is learning to organize her random, disorganized reactions into organized expressions called feelings.

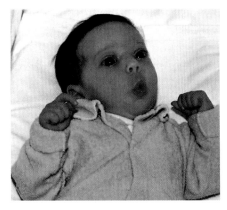 Like all learning, this takes repetition and reinforcement from the outside. When you mirror back your baby's smile, or imitate her gurgle, you are acknowledging that she has felt a real feeling and communicated it properly. When she gets her feeling across to you successfully over and over again, she can begin to take it for granted. She knows that feeling. It has gone into her emotional memory bank, the limbic system.

What goes for smiles, goes for all the other feelings that take place in that first tumultuous and exciting year. Your baby is also learning language. And she needs to have names for her emotions, so that later she can communicate them to you with words. Naming her feelings helps her learn an emotional vocabulary. For example, as you return your baby's smile, say "Oh, what a happy smile. You're so happy."

This is an interactive process. Even though a newborn doesn't have a wide range of emotional expressions, you won't be able to accurately name them. Happy and angry will cover the bases at first, but as you get to know your baby, you'll be surprised by how much variety she will introduce. With her facial expressions, her body language and her vocalizations, she'll give you bored, hungry, uncomfortable, angry, sad, lonely, surprised, excited and many other variations before she can talk.

Babies bring out the performers in us, causing us to mirror back to them what we think they are feeling, so they can see it outside themselves and learn it. Their feelings are so pure that you'll find yourself enjoying your responses with refreshing intensity.

The opportunity to register basic emotions in their brain circuits will never be as rich as it is in the first two years of their life. After birth, neurons are available to make networks and circuits. But the ones that aren't used are pruned away over time, in a kind of housekeeping effort to leave room for the active cells. If certain neurons aren't stimulated before the big clean out, they lose their ability to receive the emotional message. A severely emotionally-deprived baby seems blunted and subdued because she hasn't been shown the full range of feelings. She's missed her chance to experience some subtle tones of emotion.

Fortunately, babies are emotional geniuses, always finding ways to make us teach them more emotions. Just reacting spontaneously to their fresh, contagious moods will give them what they need.

baby's feelings

Research suggests that babies are born with a very basic set of feelings. Ultrasound has shown fetal facial expressions that look just like our expressions of disgust, sadness, happiness and fear. Just as red, blue and yellow can be combined to make an infinite number of colors, our primary feelings of sadness, anger, fear and happiness are the basis of an infinite number of emotions. Feeling and understanding a broad range of emotions enriches life.

Because infants are so responsive, they are extremely receptive to emotional cues. Frequently they will pick up the mood of another child or caregiver just because they are exposed to it. Children's moods can be as contagious as the chicken pox. Even under the age of one, if one child cries, another may offer her security blanket. This indicates that babies are learning about emotions from the very beginning of human contact.

> Before I got married I had six theories about bringing up children. Now I have six children and no theories.
>
> JOHN WILMOT

Later in life, this ability to feel what another person feels becomes the basis for developing empathy. When empathy is fully developed, it enables your child to know how others feel by drawing on her own experience of that feeling. Empathy is essential to the development of morality. Even though babies aren't sophisticated enough to empathize, cultivating their emotional responsiveness and awareness prepares them to learn empathy later.

Before a baby can develop empathy, she has to be treated empathetically by her caregivers. The key component to providing empathetic care is correctly identifying and responding to your baby's feelings and needs. This skill comes more easily to some parents than others, but with experience, you can become more and more adept at reading your baby's signals. Careful observation, quick response, and trial and error will serve you well here.

Watch your baby carefully. When she sends a signal – through a smile, a whimper, a wave of the arms or a jerk of her abdomen – tell her what you think she is telling you, and then respond in the way you think is best. If you do this consistently, she will assume that this is reality, and as she develops her abilities, she will try to do the same thing. It is never too soon to start being attentive and empathetic toward your baby.

Being empathetic means watching, recognizing and letting your baby know that you know how she feels. Even when she is a newborn, before she can talk or make meaningful eye contact, you will have the impulse to mimic her expressions and respond to her cries. When she has her first immunization shot, you won't shriek with pain to show solidarity, but you will look at her and wince, just as she is feeling the pain of the needle. She will immediately know that you feel what she feels, and that you understand each other. Because of your empathy, the baby has a chance to pass some of her anxiety over to you, the senior partner, which will ease things for her.

three steps for communicating feelings to your baby

1. Observe your baby carefully, as if you were an emotional detective. Look for all the signals — facial expression, tone of voice, physical movement and body posture.

2. Describe out loud which feeling you think your baby is experiencing. "You're kicking so hard you must be angry!" or "You're crying but I just fed you, so I don't think you're hungry. Maybe you're lonely and you'd like me to hold you."

3. Follow up with a response to your emotional interpretation. "Now that I've picked you up, you're not crying. That's better. You're so clever for telling me what you wanted."

the senses

At birth, your newborn uses her five senses to stay close to you. These senses are the compass she uses to orient herself outside the womb. Although you know where your baby is and how to find her, she does not yet have the ability to find you. The senses are five links to caregivers that give a baby the feeling of security needed for emotions to grow.

the sense of smell

By three days after birth, a breastfed baby can distinguish her mother's bra from another mother's by using her nose. The newborn sense of smell is a very useful tool, particularly because focused eyesight and language aren't yet developed.

the sense of taste

Babies are born with a preference for a sweet taste which is present in breast milk. Happy tastebuds add to the baby's pleasure in nursing, whether by breast or by bottle. Enjoying being nourished is a deeply satisfying way for babies to feel secure and connected to their caregivers. However, giving babies extra sugar, corn syrup or honey in their formula, water or other food is not a good idea. Giving babies sweet juices in their bottles as a go-to-sleep ritual has been the cause of many dental problems.

the sense of hearing

In utero, a baby hears the sounds of her mother's body and her voice. In the third trimester, she even becomes accustomed to some external sounds such as the barking of a dog, or other regular household noises such as vacuums or dishwashers. She can't understand or interpret what she hears, but it is part of her environment, and after birth those same sounds help to provide her with bearings in her new world. She needs to hear her mother's voice and the voices of her intimate caregivers from the start. Speaking gently, in a soft, slow, high-pitched singsong voice will add to your baby's sense of security and reassure her of your presence. Babies like steady, familiar sounds, even at high volume, and can even fall asleep in a noisy atmosphere if the noises are consistent. But they find sudden, piercing sounds – or unexpected silences – startling and disruptive.

"When the mind is thinking, it is talking to itself"

PLATO

the sense of sight

Newborns can follow an object with their eyes as long as it is close enough. Until their eye muscles strengthen, they are extremely nearsighted and focus best on an object ten to twelve inches from the bridge of their nose. When you hold or feed your baby, you instinctively hold her about that distance from your face, giving her the chance to study you and "learn" your face. Babies become more alert at the sight of a human face, which shows that they are developing the visual skills they need to recognize their loved ones and their fellow humans right from birth. To let your baby study your face, hold her close or lean right over her so she can see you. Being held and using sight go together at first, so that the baby is in a visual and a physical embrace.

the sense of touch

There is something magical in what your touch can do for a baby. Being cradled skin to skin with the mother right after birth allows lactation to begin more readily. Premature babies in incubators make better progress when they are stroked and when they are held skin to skin by their mothers or fathers. After the cozy container of the womb, babies feel very undefined in open air. The gentle pressure of being held gives them a secure sense of their physical bodies. Many new parents also find holding their baby relaxing, because they know that they are near the baby if she needs something.

TIPS
and techniques to stimulate your baby's senses

- Hold your baby as much as possible, including times when you are not feeding or changing her, or even when she's sleeping. As long as your hands are free, you can hold your baby. You can carry your baby in a sling or a baby snugly at times when you need your hands. Let your baby's other parent or caregiver hold the baby when you can't. Holding the baby skin to skin, in a warm environment is very beneficial.

- Talk frequently to your baby, using a gentle, slow, singsong voice with upward intonation. This stimulates brain development. In addition to talking to her, let her hear your voice by reading and singing to her.

- Make eye contact with your baby. Let her study your face, but only hold her gaze until she turns away; don't force your baby to look at you by turning her face or changing her position. When you see that she is initiating eye contact, return her gaze and talk to her enthusiastically while you look into her eyes. Change the distance between your face and hers by holding her at arm's length, then moving her closer until you are forehead to forehead.

baby's cry

A baby's cry is not a beautiful, melodious sound because it is meant to create an urgent sense that help is needed. It is remarkably effective, however, and parents since time immemorial have been debating the best ways to respond to it.

For the sake of your baby's emotional well-being, an immediate and sensitive response is absolutely essential. Your baby's cry is a plea for help and whether it is caused by hunger pains, diaper rash, or a need to be held and comforted, it is first and foremost a request for human contact. In one study, infant researchers went to crying babies and checked their diapers. If the diapers were dry, they left them on, but if the diapers were wet, they took

> Love cures people; both the ones who give it and the ones who receive it.
>
> DR. KARL MENNINGER

them off and then put the wet diapers back on. The babies with the wet diapers still stopped crying. It wasn't only the wetness that made them cry, but the desire to be picked up by their caregivers. Picking up your baby is the first step to stopping her cries. Sometimes that won't be enough, and she will continue to cry until you find the cause of her distress. But she will still start to feel better as soon as you pick her up.

The cry is also a very important form of pre-verbal communication. Your baby is trying to tell you something with her voice, and by responding promptly, you teach her that telling you something with her voice works. You've given her the feeling that she's "talked" to you, and this motivates her to continue communicating.

For this reason, we have the impulse to respond to infant cries with adult words. While you are tending to your baby, tell her what you're doing and how you're interpreting her cries. She will learn that words are a response to tears, and as she learns to talk, she will follow your example and try to use her words to tell you what's wrong. Letting your baby communicate her feelings of being distressed is one of the most important things a caregiver can do to foster healthy emotional development.

Showing her that you hear her cry and welcome the message she's giving you is deeply reassuring. In the long run, this leads to less crying because your baby is happier and more secure.

Fortunately, as babies develop, they cry less. The amount of time a baby cries peaks at around six weeks. But crying continues throughout childhood – and into adulthood – so it is important to develop a positive approach to crying from the start. Your child needs you when she cries.

You will be able to detect different sounding cries coming from your baby and, with some trial and error, will learn what they mean. A cry of pain sounds different from a cry of hunger or a cry to be held. Cries vary in pitch, frequency and intensity, but all come from the same important impulse to let you know that she wants something. Think of your baby's cries as a singing telegram, each tune conveying a different need. If you can name that tune – the hunger tune, the boredom tune, the pick-me-up tune – you will see your baby's cry as her part in communicating her needs to you.

if your baby's cries were words:

 • Pain: the cry starts with a gasp or a jagged breath, then the sound rises in a spike until the next breath. She's saying, "Help! Help! SOS!"

 • Hunger: the cry starts with a protest-like blast, intense vibration and has impressive force for the size of the baby. She's saying, "Where's my food? I want it NOW!"

 • Discontent, boredom and loneliness: a whimpering tone with a more pleading note, less vibration, but more resonance. She's saying, "Something's wrong. Can you help me? Are you there?"

Sometimes, you may find that you can't name that tune, and no matter what you try, your baby keeps on crying. This can become extremely frustrating and distressing, particularly during the first few weeks of the baby's life, when everything is so new and mysterious. But this is a normal, empathetic response to your baby. Feeling agitated by your baby's crying is a way of understanding how she is feeling. Before babies have words to tell us their feelings, they have non-verbal ways of helping us feel their emotional states. Just after giving birth, mothers have a heightened sensitivity to feelings. That can mean that they are easily stressed, but it also means they are receptive to their infant's cues.

Ongoing, shrill, inconsolable crying is very stressful, but you can increase your tolerance by remembering its emotional purpose. If you can accept the crying sound calmly while checking what the problem is, you give your baby the sense that her crying doesn't distress you. She

gains the security of having a resilient, sturdy caregiver. When she feels shaky, she knows that you will be her strength. When and how this happens can't be pinpointed to a particular day or month, but your ongoing, relaxed presence gets the point across. Your baby learns that all her emotions are acceptable.

Think of yourself as an intercom system, in which the crying baby is on "send" and you're on "receive." By calmly receiving the message, you put your own emotions aside long enough to focus on your baby's feelings. You are not pretending the cry doesn't bother you, but you are managing your response so that it isn't preventing you from concentrating. This is particularly important for handling emergencies, which can arise as children take the risks they should take to explore the world.

When your baby is crying, it helps to remember that all babies cry. In the first two years of life, babies are working extraordinarily hard at developing, learning, acquiring skills and growing, and it takes a fighting spirit to keep trying despite the inevitable setbacks of infancy. Your baby will have a cry of frustration and indignation that expresses how challenging life can be for her. This little spark of aggression (think of it as assertiveness), is needed to keep her actively learning, and when you hear it, it is your chance to admire her persistence and rejoice in her growing power to learn from experience.

Tips and techniques for coping with your baby's crying

- Go to your baby as soon as the crying begins; rapid response results in less crying.

- Talk to your baby while you try to help; use a cheerful, confident and evenly paced voice.

- Investigate each time in the same order, so your baby develops a sense of routine. For example, is she hungry? Does she want to be held or rocked? Check her diaper. Maybe she just wants company. Each baby has different needs and will tend to cry for different reasons. You will get a sense of what bothers your baby most.

- Feed your baby whenever she lets you know she's hungry. This way she will develop a recognizable hunger rhythm which will help you know when her crying is about food and when it's not.

- Soothe all her senses; speak to her gently; hold her securely; look at her lovingly and kiss her softly.

- Even if you can't stop the crying, stay with your baby and hold her or give her to your partner to hold. Whatever else she needs, she clearly needs your company.

- If the crying is making you anxious or upset, get someone to take over and take a break. Start arranging for a little time off and rest as a regular part of your schedule.

baby's gaze

Babies are born with eyes that are much larger in proportion to their faces than their other features, giving them that "wide-eyed" look that parents find irresistible. Your earliest conversations with your baby will be spoken into those entrancing eyes.

Looking into your baby's eyes with a loving expression not only teaches her to recognize you and smile at your face, but also creates another form of dialogue and a vocabulary of non-verbal expressions. When your expression mirrors hers, it confirms her feeling and solidifies her sense of herself. It also gives her the sense that she can start communication with you by looking at you and looking away from you. This helps a baby learn the difference between "me" and "not me" which she is not aware of at birth, and gradually gives her the sense that she has some control over her part of the partnership. You will notice within a few weeks that your baby will be able to attract your gaze and turn away from it just by averting her eyes, and you will get great satisfaction from this visual communication between the two of you.

Your gaze is also important in giving your baby a strong sense of security during times of distress or discomfort. Babies can go from one intense emotional state to another very quickly, as they experience a sudden pain, or are startled by a strange face, or frustrated in some way. Looking up to see your calm, confident expression and direct eye contact reminds her that your ongoing support is always available, and increases the sense of a secure base she needs to keep exploring the unknown.

During your baby's settled periods, eye contact between the two of you is like an invitation to join the big wide world, to move from self-absorption to looking outward. Your gaze initiates socializing, first with you and eventually with others. Although newborns do not focus beyond eight to ten inches at birth, they prefer the sight of a face, and appear to be looking into the eyes of the one who holds them. They are ready for "eye talk."

Babies use their gaze long before they master words, or even begin to make vocalizing sounds. But even once they are talking, their eyes and the interchange with their parents' eyes will remain a powerful mode of communication. The disapproving glance that stops them from touching something forbidden; the doting smile that greets them when they get up from a nap; the shared sparkle of glee at the sight of something beloved is a non-verbal dialogue between parent and child. This teaches your baby how to "read" non-verbal cues in others, and how to "send" non-verbal cues. These are extremely important communication and social skills.

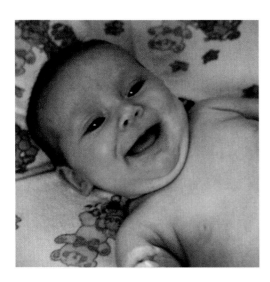

POINTS TO REMEMBER

■ Brain development continues after birth.

■ Babies need stimulation for their brains and feelings to develop.

■ Babies learn basic emotions through interaction with caregivers.

■ Talking to your baby stimulates brain development.

■ Newborns use their five senses to stay close to their caregivers.

■ Babies use their gaze to start and end eye contact and as a form of non-verbal communication.

■ All babies cry.

■ Babies cry to communicate; it is essential to respond to crying at once.

■ Learning to handle a crying baby calmly minimizes distress in the caregiver and the infant.

the timing of emotional development

Emotional growth follows a basic pattern, but differs with each individual. As your baby develops physically and cognitively, her increased interaction with the world exposes her to new emotional challenges. However, the basic theme remains the same – finding a way to become independent while still feeling securely connected to her caregivers. This emotional project goes on for a lifetime, but is particularly intense during childhood.

Humans have a built-in drive toward emotional independence and a built-in need to stay connected to other humans. Learning how to be separate from you physically, and connected to you emotionally at the same time, is an internal process that you can't see, but it is ongoing. You will notice tentative steps, unexpected leaps and frustrating setbacks, but little by little, your dependent baby becomes an independent person. What follows is the emotional work your baby is doing during her first two years.

getting settled in the first two months

The transition from womb to world seems to take everything a baby has for the first couple of months of life. The physical processes of eating, sleeping and eliminating need time to settle into a pattern. To a newborn's parents, it seems that managing these functions is all there is time to do or think about. But emotional development is also taking place.

The baby depends on your presence and management. When you are there, minimizing distress and helping her create a regular routine, your baby gradually develops a sense that she works a certain way, sleeping at certain times, being alert at others, eating according to her needs, and so on. This pattern changes with growth, and your attention assists in those changes of pattern.

But even though she has the equipment to develop stronger means of identifying you as her special caregiver, she does not yet have the sophistication to know the difference between herself and someone else. A baby does not know where she ends and you begin anymore than she did when she was in utero. First, she needs a sense of her own physical rhythm before she can recognize that she is also a separate person.

A newborn goes from being part of her mother's body to being a separate body. It takes time for her to "learn" that she is in a separate body from her mother, and that her mother is in a separate body from the other caregivers in her life. It is best that the newborn has a chance to learn this from a few steady caregivers, such as her mommy, daddy and one other adult. Too many caregivers overwhelm the baby with too many smells, sounds, faces and holds.

The womb is not a highly stimulating environment, and a newborn's environment should be equally calm. New mothers also need a smoothly running, undemanding environment at this time. As well as forging their own relationship with the baby, fathers have to play a major role in controlling the household and in minimizing intrusion on the mother and baby. Babies generate a lot of social traffic and sometimes an extra adult is needed to be the traffic cop. The three of you need a lot of privacy to enjoy the intimacy of this time.

 **and techniques for dads in the first two months**

- Create the emotional support for your partner by communicating with her on the help that she needs.

- If your baby is being breastfed, and mom has to get up frequently at night, help her make up the lost sleep by taking a complete shift between feedings. If a breast pump is being used, or if the baby is being bottlefed, work out a shared feeding schedule.

- Be the social director and protect your newborn and her mommy from invasion by well-meaning but exhausting visitors.

- Pick one special baby job that will be yours and yours alone to do for the first eight weeks, such as bathing the baby or holding her at a certain time each day. Share other jobs, such as changing and rocking.

- Put extra effort into being the baby observer during this time. Mom will be tired but you can be as alert as ever, and take note of your newborn's many traits and qualities.

- Be the family historian. Keep notes, photos or videos.

- Wear the baby in a carrier on your chest. This gives mom a break and lets the baby get nice and close so she can smell you, hear your heart and get used to what you feel like.

- Let the baby nap on your chest.

learning to soothe herself

The most willing parents in the world will occasionally have to attend to things besides their beloved newborn, and all babies are faced with the dilemma of feeling a need when no one is there to help satisfy it. Each baby finds her own way to cope. If the cry and the gaze don't summon the attention she craves, she will find her own ways of comforting herself, such as sucking her thumb.

Newborns have an extremely powerful urge to suck even when they are not actively hungry. A baby who is already full may still need to suck on something. Most babies find their own way to fulfill this need. Many babies begin sucking their fingers or thumbs while still in the womb, and discover this way of soothing themselves once they are born. This behavior provides them with important comfort and teaches them a way to meet their own need with their own body. It should not be discouraged.

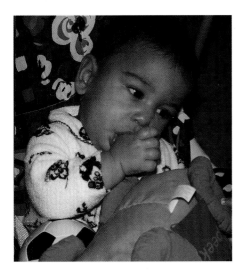

Many parents worry that finger or thumb-sucking will be bad for their baby's dental formation and cause orthodontic problems. Dentists now agree that early sucking habits are not problematic. Generally, children give up these habits spontaneously before age five, as long as adults don't interfere or become punitive about it.

Most breastfed babies can get enough sucking when they are nursing, if they are allowed to suck even after they have emptied the breast. The urge to suck varies from baby to baby. There will be some babies who don't choose to suck their fingers, but in addition to sucking at the breast and bottle, need to suck more. A pacifier could be the answer for these babies. You may also see your baby suck the end of a blanket or part of a toy. Be very careful that anything she might suck on cannot come away in a small piece and result in choking.

comforting your newborn

A crib can't hold your baby as snugly as a womb or as securely as your arms. In the first eight weeks, when your baby is still a "little bundle" she needs to be wrapped up like one, and put into a smaller cradle or bassinet. Putting the bassinet near your bed also allows her to smell you, hear you breathe and feel as close as possible to you even when she is asleep. Most mammals sleep with their young, and keeping your newborn in your room will not prevent her from learning to sleep independently later.

A stuffed animal and a baby blanket are items which your baby can become familiar with and possibly turn to for comfort at times. Newborns are preparing themselves to become social beings by growing emotionally attached to their caregivers. Being with your baby as much as possible in these weeks sows the seeds for healthy sociability.

POINTS TO REMEMBER

- Be a baby observer to learn your own baby's unique traits and characteristics.
- Babies may develop an intense attachment to an object they find soothing to hold, touch and stroke.
- Baby's fulfill their own urge to suck, even when they're not hungry, e.g., sucking their thumb.

two months to six months: growing attachment

Once your baby settles into a regular pattern, she has longer periods to be alert and focused on things other than her bodily functions. This is when she can begin to really interact with the world, using each new skill as it develops. This gives your baby more ways to relate to you and her loved ones, further intensifying her attachment and adding new feelings to it. During this exciting developmental period you can celebrate many strides as she takes them. She has a growing sense of control over her body and a comfortable familiarity with her routine. She gradually becomes aware that she is separate from you, although she still depends utterly on your being there for a sense of well-being.

It's important to help your baby feel included in family life. It may appear that she isn't getting much out of a routine activity, but for your baby it is togetherness that counts. She begins to take it as a matter of course that you do things together because she wants to be your partner, and life seems richer and happier that way. As she spends this time with you, she absorbs a sense that you are not only at her side, but actually part of her. She gains confidence because she's secure, knowing you're there.

One way to make sure that your baby is always included is to carry her in a sling on your hip or a holder that goes across your chest. Many parents reserve these carriers for trips outside the house, but it is also a good idea to carry your baby with you during your routine activities at home.

> Tell me and I will forget, show me, and I may remember. Involve me, and I will understand.
>
> ANCIENT PROVERB

 **and techniques for including your baby**

- Take time off from tasks in the home to pay total attention to your baby. Schedule this for the same time every day, preferably when you're not too tired.

- When doing housework, try to concentrate on one room at a time so you can settle the baby in a spot where she can see you, and then move her along with you when you go to another room.

- Set up secondary "baby stations" in rooms where you spend a lot of time, so your baby has a sense of her space in that room. For example, leave a basket of toys and a blanket on the floor in the living room, so she can play while you watch television. Have a playmat with her own set of measuring cups and spoons in the kitchen – a safe distance from the stove and out of the line of foot traffic.

- Get an answering machine for the telephone, so that if it rings when you can't leave the baby, you will be able to call back. Indicate in your greeting that you might be home but just busy, so feel free to try again.

learning to eat solid foods

Whether your baby is bottle or breastfed, you will eventually add solid foods to her diet. By this point, your baby knows that her mouth is a wonderful entry point for good sensations. She puts anything she can into her mouth – a nipple, her thumb and fingers – and gets a great deal of pleasure. So keep anything small enough to choke on, out of reach.

It is important to add solid foods to her collection of mouth pleasures long before you remove the bottle or breast. The tastebuds will work their own magic and interest your child in a new way of eating. The main goal is as much to invite her to find pleasure in solid foods as it is to increase her nutritional options. This is the first step in learning to eat as part of the group at a table, which is a major social and emotional experience.

For this reason, learning to eat solid food from a spoon must be fun. With your pediatrician's advice, select a starter food, such as rice cereal. Put a tiny amount on a baby spoon and hold it to your baby's lips. Watch closely – this is a real turning point. It's hard to imagine, but your baby has no reason to know what a spoon is used for or what the mush on top of it could do for her. At first, your baby will suck a small taste of the cereal through mostly closed lips. If the flavor appeals, she will look like she's ready for more. Little by little, you can insert the spoon through the lips, but not very far, very fast. If it's too far, the baby will gag; too close to the front of the mouth, and the food will dribble away before she gets a taste. You need to carefully position the spoon just far enough inside the mouth so that she can get the food and swallow it. Gentle exploration is the way.

If she turns her head away, clamps her mouth shut, or just seems indifferent, don't pursue it. Leave it to try again later. Coaxing your baby to eat will be frustrating for you, and will communicate to her that you need her to eat for your sake, not hers. Spoon-feeding is team work, and you need two willing team members. To develop a sensitivity to what it feels like for your baby, have someone spoon-feed you several spoonfuls of something you don't like when you're not hungry.

Babies are notoriously messy eaters, even when you are the one manipulating the food. They want to touch, smell, spread, examine and taste the food. It is very important that they be allowed to explore eating in their own way, and that they see you take pleasure in their explorations. If a baby senses that you are not happy with the way she eats, food can become something with the power to upset you.

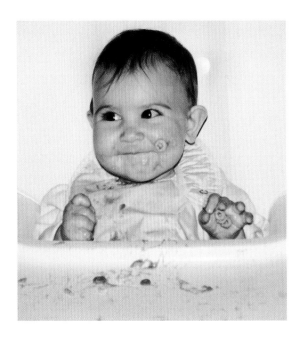

POINTS TO REMEMBER

- It is important to help your baby feel included in the family - keep her with you as much as possible during daily routines.

- Keep anything small enough to choke on out of reach.

- Learning to eat from a spoon should be fun so that she finds pleasure in solid foods.

six months to one year: from infancy to toddlerhood

Human development is designed so that as your baby gains the physical ability to move away from you in space – by crawling and eventually walking – she adds the psychological skill of holding an image of you in her mind, so that she still doesn't feel completely alone. In order to separate physically, she has to attach emotionally, and by around six months, that attachment is really taking shape. She becomes increasingly confident that her special caregiver is there for her, so that she can venture away when her curiosity draws her elsewhere.

This greater recognition of your unique role in her life also introduces the awareness that other people are not you. She may begin to show reluctance to be with strangers who try to get too close, and may become clingy, especially when other people disturb her exclusive monopoly over you. This is an inevitable development which varies in intensity from child to child. Sometimes this phase can make life tricky for parents who suddenly find that they can't leave their baby with a sitter or don't understand why she is burying her face in her hands when well-meaning friends approach. It does not last forever, and is actually an important change.

As your baby begins to crawl, she will inevitably discover that sometimes she moves herself right out of your sight when she had no intention of doing so. This new mobility is a bit unsettling if it means mom refuses to remain visible no matter where she chooses to go. So she may direct all her movements to following you, and become extremely sensitive to being apart from you even though she tolerated it relatively well in the weeks before crawling. It's as if she's been given the keys to a car but doesn't know it can go into reverse as well as drive, and she isn't sure how she'll get back to you if she moves away. This unexpected clinging may seem like a step backwards to you, but with emotional development, such behaviors are temporary and provide a needed pause before the next leap in development. You can ease this period by calling out to her in a playful singsong voice from wherever you happen to be.

When your baby begins to be shy around strangers, it is a sign that her sense of separateness is growing. This heightened understanding that she is an independent being creates great excitement and joy in your child, but also makes her realize that you can be physically absent, and she begins to miss you. Even though she can start to keep a mental image of you in her head when she chooses to depart from you, it doesn't mean she feels comfortable when you choose to leave her.

As she moves from infancy to toddlerhood, with the development of walking and talking, her emotional task is to become comfortable when she is apart from you by keeping her link to you alive in her mind. No baby achieves this without effort, but every baby succeeds eventually to some degree.

Many babies have one special possession which they take comfort in touching, stroking and holding. Usually it is something they have had with them from their earliest days, and it feels cuddly and smells familiar. It could be a baby blanket, a stuffed animal, a soft towel or the lining of a coat. By holding it, stroking it and sleeping with it, a baby becomes extremely attached to this special possession. Because it is portable, she can take it with her wherever she goes, and eventually insists on it.

This object gives your baby something to hang on to when she can't hang on to you. It takes on such soothing abilities that it seems to have magic power, and she may become inseparable from it, even when you are together. This varies from child to child. Some children never develop a need for this treasure. Others take their stuffed animal off to sleepover camp when they are ten, and even to college when they are 18. But if your little one does have a beloved possession, there is no harm in encouraging it. It is a sign of progress from being attached inside the womb, to being physically connected through holding, to standing separately with the aid of a beloved prop. You can take pride in her emotional growth.

Letting your child see that you know she needs "Mr. Bear" to fall asleep shows her that you understand a very deep and private feeling. At the same time, show her that you regard this as her special private possession which you do not own or control. Never grab it away, remove it as punishment, hand it to another sibling or force her to share it. Wash it as little as possible, as it builds up a smell that is very comforting to your baby. And don't set a time limit on how old she will be when she gives it up.

Most of all, guard your baby's treasured object carefully, especially if your toddler wants to take it out of the house.

> "The best and most beautiful things in the world cannot be seen, nor touched... but are felt in the heart."
>
> HELEN KELLER

 **and techniques for helping your baby separate from you**

- In new situations, hold your child until she indicates that she wants to be put down. If she is walking or standing, hold her hand until she decides to let go.

- Let your child "hide" by putting her head down or draping a bath towel over her head, and then ask out loud, "Where is she?" with great wonderment. When she reveals herself, act joyfully surprised and have a wonderful reunion.

- Talk to your child while you are face to face, and then move gradually away while still talking so that she sees that she can still hear you. Do this playfully for practice at first.

- Keep your child informed of where you are, especially if she is confined to a high chair or crib and can't follow you. Explain that you will be right back and come back as promised.

- Introduce your child to substitute caregivers gradually. Start by having them care for her in your presence, so they move from being a stranger to a friend who follows the same routines as you do.

enriching the bond

Helping your baby feel connected to you while she moves beyond your immediate presence will give her confidence. In these early months of exploration, she is simultaneously examining the world and testing your presence. This may not be apparent to the naked eye, and your baby may seem to be blithely setting forth. The reason she looks so confident is that she knows you are there. She is not as independent as she looks. All babies need to feel that their caregivers are still steadfastly present in case of emergency. At first, she can only have this secure feeling by checking that you are still there. But eventually, if you are available whenever she checks, she will develop a portable "inner parent." She will feel as if you are part of her, and she won't even think about it. The more solid her sense of you is during her first year, the more confident and resilient your child will be.

What makes that sense of you really solid is the countless number of positive interactions that have taken place between the two of you since her birth. In particular, her feeling that you understand what she needs and know how to provide it even if she can't tell you, gives her the sense that she has a secure base. It's not just the quantity of your interactions, but the quality.

Parents instinctively want to provide tender loving care. The most crucial aspect of that love is a desire and ability to understand your child's feelings and to give her appropriate responses. Knowing that somebody else feels the way you do, without being told, is a wonderful experience and the basis of deep affection. Great friendships and marriages build on it, and your new partnership with your baby depends on the strength of this communication.

It depends, initially, on your ability to share and empathize with your child's many states and feelings, and to reflect them back at the same level of intensity. When your baby puts the final ring on her ring toy, she needs you to clap with satisfaction that matches her internal feeling of satisfaction. If she's ecstatic, she needs you to reflect back that ecstatic feeling. If she's mildly encouraged, she needs you to react mildly. You can convey your response to her by taking her feeling and expressing it in a different way. If she smiles, you clap. If her eyes twinkle, you say "wow!" Emotions are expressed verbally and physically. You take her feeling and translate it. Then she can see you understand her, and her feelings make sense. When a baby and a caregiver's spontaneous reactions are well matched, it gives the baby a sense of emotional harmony.

Empathy consists of recognizing another person's emotional state and feeling it enough to imitate it back. Children actually begin to learn empathy by imitating the feelings of others. A baby may smile simply because she sees you smile – she is empathizing with you and imitating you. But when you get a jolt of joy from that smile and return it with something extra, such as an enthusiastic verbal comment like, "What a smile!" you are matching and enhancing the feelings. When your baby reaches for the ball dangling from her mobile and can't quite connect, and you say, "Stretch – stre-e-etch" in an extended tone that mimics what she's doing with her body, you are using sounds to communicate to her that you understand what she's doing and how it feels. You are being a partner in her enterprise, and every time you are emotionally matched, her sense of security is intensified. Countless subtle acts of understanding go into her emotional memory and create one solid concept of a loving parent.

And vice versa. Your baby tries to understand you as much as you want to empathize with her. If you laugh during a conversation on the telephone, she may break into her own giggle and wave her hands at you. If you cry in alarm when you accidentally hurt yourself, she will be alert and attentive to you. She will use her emotional knowledge to let you know she understands you because her desire is to give back the love you've given her, and to be an equal emotional partner. Always remain aware that babies are reading your emotional condition and reactions and learning from them.

Empathy comes naturally to most of us, but we differ in degree of skill. As a new parent, you are called upon to understand a far less-equipped individual than you've had to understand in the past, and at first it can be confusing.

the social creature

In the first half of the second year, while your baby works on beginning to walk and talk, she is becoming increasingly interested in other people. This is when she can join the larger family circle as an equal member included in outings, sitting at meals, and visiting close friends and family. Although she may feel anxious when others approach her too forwardly, she will indicate when she is ready to approach them. And the entire time she is in a social setting, she will be observing and learning about people.

Babies take particular joy from watching other babies, although they do not play with each other in the way that older children do. However, they get a lot from being in the park with the kids, or having a baby friend come over and sit on the same blanket with toys while their mothers talk. This exposure is a rich curriculum of language, social and emotional skills which your absorbent little sponge is eager to soak up.

The key to introducing your baby to the social world is to pace the exposure to her speed. A baby who enjoys visits from grandma and playing with the baby down the block

doesn't necessarily feel ready to go to the library baby program and face twenty babies and caregivers sitting in a circle. Start by bringing the world to your baby bit by bit, then broaden her exposure to the outside world in small doses. Take your cues from her.

Taking her along as your companion when you have errands is a good way to start, but don't expect to get as much done as in the past. A trip to the grocery store, where you run into a friend and chat, and then browse through aisle-upon-aisle of brightly packaged objects, could be too stimulating for your baby. Several short trips, with modest goals, are far more suitable, even if they are not nearly as efficient.

the child-friendly environment

With every physical and cognitive stride your baby takes, she will want to touch, taste, smell, grab and look at more and more of the world. Thwarting that impulse would prevent her from learning and loving the world, but keeping her safe is your job because she needs your judgment. You have no choice but to limit some of your little explorer's activities. Open conflict and a war of wills can develop if this isn't handled delicately, in a way that is appropriate to her development. Forbidding exploration and trying to impose stern discipline is counter-productive and ineffective at this age. It asks the baby to understand the concept of limits and to take responsibility for herself before she is cognitively or emotionally ready. And it establishes an adversarial relationship between you and your budding explorer, just when you want her to feel that you are her most trusted ally.

Later in life, you will have to teach your child about limits and self-discipline, but for now, all you can do is protect your child from harm by removing the harm wherever possible.

POINTS TO REMEMBER

- In the first year, babies begin to differentiate between you and other intimate caregivers or strangers.

- Babies cannot be empathetic, but preparation for empathy begins in infancy. Attentive, understanding care provides a model for children to imitate as they grow.

- Protect your child from harm by creating a safe environment for exploration.

the second year: a testing toddler

The second year of life is as dramatic in its own way as the first. At the beginning of the first year, the fetus is thrust into babyhood. Sometime in the second year, the baby begins to walk and is thrust into vertical mobility. Instinct drives the toddler to use her newfound ability to explore a world that looks different and is tantalizingly accessible. The toddler is in the grip of an irresistible urge to explore.

But the need to feel close to you does not go away – it is as strong as her need to explore. Teaching her how to find a balance between these two extremes is the challenge.

Toddlers may be a challenge, but they are also exciting, high-spirited companions. They are thrilled by their discoveries, and they show you the world through fresh eyes. You may find this period one of the most delightful and gratifying of your years as a parent. Appreciating your toddler for the imaginative, curious perspective she brings to everyday life is the key to enjoying this turbulent stage. By being supportive, you will guide her through the dips and valleys she encounters as she becomes an independent being.

In the first year of life, you established a strong link with your baby, and this enables her to carry an inner sense that there is someone watching over her. This inner guardian is not only her growing concept of you, but a blend of feelings, reactions and memories drawn from her relationship with all her significant caregivers. It is a good sense of trust that she envisions by thinking of you, but it is her version of you, and it is an ever-changing image.

"If you love something set it free. If it comes back, it is yours – if it doesn't, it never was."

ANONYMOUS

While you tended to her simpler needs in babyhood, she built an extremely positive image of you. But when your toddler challenges you, as part of her development, things become more complicated.

Toddlers need physical protection as they use their new skills, but aren't thankful for the limits you impose. Toddlers throw themselves into their projects body and soul, and can be extremely willful about doing what they want – and not doing what you want. "No" is a word that comes easily to toddlers'  lips. Toddlers are not trying to make your life difficult, but their development demands that they assert themselves. As the senior partner, you will have to manage schedules, choose activities, establish safe limits, teach acceptable behavior and prevent accidents. Your toddler will feel that something has changed between you and her, but she won't understand exactly what. She doesn't know that she's changed. Even as her curiosity and mobility drive her forward into new territory, her baby self yearns for the security of the crib.

Keeping things as positive as possible, while remaining confidently in control, will minimize conflict. But eventually, you will have to tell her no, and she will have to live with it. This is a very big emotional task. She loves you intensely, but you are frustrating her. How can she get what she wants without making you mad or sad? Or, how can she give up what she wants without getting mad at you? And why does there have to be such a thing as "no"? These are perplexing questions on your toddler's mind. It will take time for her to get used to the new world of rules.

Your goal is not to get her to obey out of fear of punishment or loss of your love. You want her to actively choose to cooperate because she feels that you are partners and wants to do what you want her to do. This cooperation is built on the support and understanding you gave her in the first year of her life. If she feels that you understand what she wants and needs, even when you can't let her have it, she will be more likely to accept compromise.

You and your toddler will actually negotiate because she knows that you will go at least halfway if you can.

Learning to curb her own desires in order to help another person is the beginning of moral behavior. It is a major developmental achievement and is only just beginning in the toddler. There will be many days when she can't muster cooperation, but feels like she will explode if she doesn't get her way. She wants a sense that she is in control of her life.

Wherever possible, allow her safe choices and share the control where you think the junior partner can handle it. You can even go so far, during playtime, to let her order you around. By this stage you may have become so used to making all your child's choices that you don't even see the opportunities for her to be in charge, but there are many. She can tell you which clothes she wants to wear, which fruit she wants for a snack, which story she wants you to read to her, how much water to put in the tub, and whether she wants to go to the park or just play in the yard. She can give herself a bath – under your constant supervision – and she can feed herself, even if it does mean washing her after every meal.

Jeremy's idea of a good time was to take everything out of his dresser and spread it all over the floor of his room. His mother, Irene, was fairly easy-going and let him enjoy this once or twice. The third time, however, she explained that now Jeremy had to help her put the clothes back. He said, "No, mommy do it," and ran out of the room. She went and picked him up, carried him back into the room and shut the door so he couldn't get out. She quietly began putting things in the drawer and handed Jeremy a pair of socks to put back. He threw them at her sulkily. She picked them up and put them in the drawer with a little smile, and said, "Bad socks! No fun!" Jeremy looked at her thoughtfully. She put away another pair of socks, repeating, "No fun." Then Jeremy joined her, saying, "No fun" with each effort. Irene knew he enjoyed making a mess more than cleaning it up, and Jeremy felt better when he could express this as he performed his task.

These lesser controls will compensate for the firm control you must retain as the senior partner. There is no choice when it comes to playing in traffic, hitting another toddler, playing with matches or throwing a dish. Your toddler feels more secure when she sees you are consistent and comfortable with the limits that you establish, even if she objects strenuously. Explain yourself to your toddler in terms she can understand, invite her to express herself to you, and sympathize with her when you can't give her what she wants. "I'm sorry you can't sit on my lap when I drive. We could get hurt. You have to sit in the car seat because it is safer that way." You can let her know you understand what she wants and why she wants it, even if you aren't giving it to her, and still remain in charge.

Researchers who have observed toddlers in a home setting have discovered that mild disagreement occurs once every three minutes and major conflict about three times an hour! You could be the most sensitive, accommodating parent in the world, but you'll still get opposition, so don't blame yourself. Your toddler really needs to assert herself to show you what she wants and who she is trying to become.

Just as you need to be able to handle a crying baby calmly, you need to become relaxed about your toddler's opposition. It occurs for more than one reason. Part of it is simply that she wants her way. Sometimes she has just been too frustrated by her efforts to explore and master something new. Sometimes she feels worried that she doesn't want to do what you want her to do. She doesn't know how her new drive to be her own boss will affect you. She wants to stay as close as ever and to please you as before, but she wants to go her own way.

Temper tantrums are part of this demanding emotional period, when your toddler is trying to balance between pleasing you and doing everything her own way. Tantrums are a sign of emotional struggle, and with the proper support, they can be used to develop new skills in self-control and recognize new things about the limits of reality.

A temper tantrum is like blowing an emotional fuse. Negative feelings of unexpected intensity overwhelm your toddler, throwing her into a storm of rage, anxiety, fear and misery. It may begin as a way of defying you, but it soon becomes an experience over which she has no control – she becomes possessed by her negative feelings and the actual event that caused the tantrum becomes a side issue.

Your role is to show her that her angry feelings don't hurt or distress you and that you have strength enough to spare for the both of you. You don't have to actually end the tantrum. Trying to end a tantrum is like trying to end a sneeze. It has to run its course. But just as you can hand your child a tissue and say, "Bless you," after the sneeze, you can support your toddler while she undergoes the scary emotional melt down of her tantrum, and show her afterward that it hasn't changed anything between you and her.

TIPS and techniques for handling temper tantrums

- Stay close to your toddler. You may want to try to embrace her, but be prepared to be pushed away. Your toddler is struggling between needing you and needing to be independent. It may help her if she can see you without you touching her.

- If your toddler is going to hurt herself or harm something, you may have to move her to a safe place.

- If you are in public, try to find a quiet spot out of the line of observation by strangers.

- If your toddler is experiencing frequent, highly distressing tantrums, keep track of when they occur. You may be able to prevent some by changing the way you're doing things. She may need more rest, less excitement, more time alone, a little more room to explore or something else that you can provide.

toddler talk

The term "toddler" refers to the wobbling, unstable steps that children this age take before they become truly competent walkers. They have begun to use their legs, but they have not mastered upright mobility. The same is true of their ability to use language. Toddlers are in possession of many words and may even be using phrases and sentences. But they have not mastered the nuance of language. In this way, trying to communicate with words can be extremely frustrating for them.

It is important to remember to speak as simply as possible to your toddler, even if she is displaying some pretty fancy vocabulary. She might have learned the word "dictionary" because grandma taught it to her one day, but still doesn't know the word "book." She may know that the neighbor's four legged pet is a "Fido" and call all canines that because she hasn't learned the word "dog."

Despite some misunderstandings, you should continue talking with her so that she can gradually adjust to your model of language. In the interim, you have to become an interpreter of your child's unique speech. It is important to encourage her to converse with you, so that she begins to feel that language is for dialogue, and words can be used to communicate needs, solve problems and find ways to work out conflict.

Language can be used for very basic negotiation. When your toddler says, "No bed, not tired," you can say, "Story now, bed after." This shows that you listen to her words and use yours to meet her part way.

Toddlers often use a word correctly even though they don't understand its meaning. They have just heard it in context and know how to put it in the same context. This leads parents to think their toddler understands more than they do. Sometimes their language is simple imitation, and it is too early for them to understand the concept behind the word.

CASE STUDY 3

Terry began talking at around a year. She said "up," "bed" and "milk" to let her mother know what she wanted, and Marcie found that made things much easier. Without noticing it, she got in the habit of cueing Terry to say "thank you" whenever she gave her something she asked for. In a slightly singsong voice she would ask, "what do you say?" whenever she gave Terry a cookie or some juice, and Terry always replied, "Thank you." Other parents were extremely impressed and Marcie was delighted. But one day, without thinking about it, she gave Terry a cookie and said, "Say thank you," and Terry did not respond. Then she realized Terry didn't really understand what she was saying, she was just following a cue. After that she concentrated on saying thank you to Terry and to other people in front of Terry, and many months later Terry began to say thank you spontaneously.

toddler socializing

Toddlers are ready to socialize with other toddlers, although they cannot yet play independently without supervision. In fact, they are more likely to play alongside, rather than interact with another toddler. Adults need to be present when toddlers play. It is an important opportunity to teach your child acceptable social behavior.

Feelings are contagious amongst toddlers, and they watch each other carefully. This is a chance to point out to your child how other people feel and how her own actions have affected other people. Toddlers are not ready to behave in a consciously empathetic manner, but they can begin to understand how other people's feelings are similar to their own, if this is pointed out to them.

TIPS and techniques for encouraging empathy

- Talk to your child about her feelings and explain how you feel as well. "You look sad when you are sick. I want you to feel better. Can I give you a cuddle?"

- Gradually and simply talk about the feelings of others. "Let's visit grandma because she's lonely," or "Joey is happy because it's her birthday."

- Compare your child's feelings to other people's feelings. "Joey cried when she got her needle, just like you did."

- If your child hurts another child by word or action, point out how the other party feels, in straightforward but not accusatory tones. "You pushed Emily and made her fall down. That hurts her and makes her sad."

- Give your child a chance to repair the damage if she does something negative, by suggesting what she can do and explaining why. "You can say you're sorry to Emily and ask her if she wants a cookie. That will cheer her up and make her see that you still want to be her friend."

POINTS TO REMEMBER

- Toddlers may learn to assert themselves by opposing their caregivers.

- Studies have shown that toddlers may disagree with their caregivers as often as once every three minutes.

- Temper tantrums are part of this demanding emotional period. Toddlers are trying to balance between pleasing you and doing everything their own way.

- Emotional development follows a basic pattern but timing differs from person to person.

building blocks for a healthy emotional base

Y ou are the senior partner in the process of building the emotional base for your child. Everything she learns from her early years sets the stage for her later development of emotional skills and interpersonal relationships.

trust

Your child's development of trust begins in the first years of dependence. As she learns that you are there to provide for her, comfort her and care for her, she uses this knowledge to develop her emotional responses. She learns how to feel and eventually learns the skills to regulate her own emotions and inner controls. You convey to her, through your words and actions, what you feel and expect and you mirror back, her own reactions. Eventually, her actions and behavior will show that she wants to please herself by pleasing you, and it will be easier for her to recognize your authority later on and relate in a healthy way to others. The ever-changing challenge is to find the balance between closeness with her and your child's need to explore her physical and emotional world. Encourage her to enjoy relationships with other family members and caregivers — these attachments will add to her growing sense of trust in others.

Dear Mother, I'm all right. Stop worrying about me.

EGYPTIAN PAPYRUS LETTER, CIRCA 2000 B.C.

personal style

Your baby has her own personal style or temperament. Her development is shaped by the interacting influences of heredity and environment. You will notice recurrent patterns of behavior, but these patterns can change at different ages and in different situations. Your baby's temperament is not within her control in the early years. The most important thing to recognize is that by watching your baby carefully and keying your responses to her, you will enhance her self-esteem and sense of security.

Your child's personal style requires you to understand her as an individual and react to her in a unique way. If you are closely tuned in to her, you will be better prepared to guide her through future significant changes and milestones.

Feeling comfortable with the fit of your personality with your child's, and learning to manage this fit, will benefit you both later as you grow and change together. Your sensitivity to your toddler's temperament and needs, communicating appropriate and clear guidelines and creating the right environment for your child to thrive in, can develop into a friendship that will last for life.

ten strategies for encouraging emotional expression

1. stay connected to your baby

Being responsive to your baby's unique cues and responding sensitively helps her learn that her impulses have meaning. Her cries bring comforting responses and good things, and you affirm her self-expression. The connected baby is far more likely to become a child who is capable of recognizing and showing deep feelings. Watch and observe your baby to help you understand her individual way of expressing herself and her needs.

2. encourage and respect toddler feelings

The expressive baby and responsive parent bring a winning combination into toddlerhood. Because her cues were listened to and decoded in the first year, your toddler

is better able to express herself. Understand that her feelings are important and healthy, and acknowledge her feelings. By recognizing and labeling them, for example, "It looks like you are really unhappy," or "I wonder if you are feeling sad," you also help your toddler to give names to her emotions.

3. share your own feelings and label them

It helps your child to understand feelings if you acknowledge and name your own feelings. Show her how you feel with your facial expressions and voice tone so that she can learn how these match up with words. She needs to learn a comfortable balance between expressing her feelings and controlling them, and she will follow your example and cues.

4. be approachable

Your toddler is a little person with big needs and a limited ability to communicate these needs. Help her by meeting her with eye-to-eye level contact and being attentive even when you don't understand what she is trying to say. With your encouraging body language, for example, nodding your head, eye contact and a comforting hand on her shoulder, you indicate that you want to listen to and understand her feelings.

5. be a good listener

Listen attentively to your toddler and match emotions with her. Knowing when to speak and when to hold back helps you to be a good listener. Give your child the time she needs to explain how she is feeling. There can be an emotional outburst first before she can find the words to talk about her feelings. Mirror your child's feelings with your facial expressions. Being empathetic toward her will give her the skills she needs to be empathetic toward others.

6. distinguish between feelings and behavior

Draw out your child's own explanation of why she feels the way she does. If you are dealing with difficult behavior in your toddler, suggest alternative behavior and try to help her express the underlying feelings. Acknowledge her feelings by trying to see the situation from her point of view, so that you can then work in your adult wisdom.

7. give help and set safe limits

Your child's emotional safety will depend on you setting the boundaries, especially if she is upset. For example, gentle but firm holding or moving to a safer physical place will give her the time and space to express herself safely. Reasonable limits will not oppress your child.

Your toddler eventually needs to learn when to ask for help. Asking for help is not only necessary for learning, but also a way of drawing closer to you. Model this by asking your toddler to help you with simple tasks, by explaining that even you need help. Helping makes a child feel needed, therefore valued, and plants the idea that helping each other is a good thing to do. Children whose parents help them gladly will be more likely to ask for help from other adults in their life, such as teachers.

8. teach your child to be sensitive to others

In order to be sensitive to others, your child must first be sensitive to herself. She must recognize her own feelings and feel comfortable expressing them, when appropriate. This is the starting point for building good relationships with others.

The most resilient children are often both responsible and nurturing. Helping others, for example, a younger sibling, promotes feelings of strength. Create the right opportunities for your child to experience this.

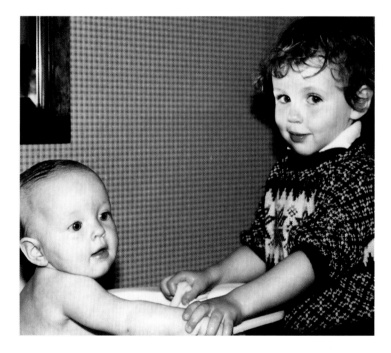

9. get support when you need it

Acknowledging your own emotions and feelings and being realistic about what you can achieve is a way to be responsive to your child's range of emotions and feelings. Ask your parenting partner and your child's other care-givers to give you the support and relief that you need.

10. be there and have fun

Your child should feel confident that she is a top priority and there are times when she has your undivided attention, for example, at bedtime, during a meal or a period of play. The ritual of a nightly bedtime story creates a reassuring routine that she can come to expect.

The delight and joy you have with your child and the mutual experiences of play will build a base for future good times and friendship. How you react to your own setbacks influences your child's resilience and ability to bounce back from problems. Have a sense of humor and show your child that learning is fun.

learning how to behave starts with love

Your child's behavior, or learning how to behave, eventually becomes internalized in her. Decide the basic principles of behavior based on the values that are important to you and your family. Your child wants to learn, to become more mature and more competent in all ways, and will do this when she is ready. As her parent, you are her guide and teacher — the one who is in control. She will learn a great deal by watching you, but of course, the goal is for her to learn self-control or inner control.

Your baby's behaviors initially are involuntary, such as crying from hunger. This is not conscious behavior. The best foundation for later behavior is early love; love which is as secure, mutual, predictable and enjoyable as you can make it.

If she experiences you as warm, loving and fulfilling her needs, she also experiences herself as these things. This is the beginning of her self-image and self-respect which will later lead to adult behavior. First she will learn to behave in ways which show that she singles you out for love. Then she will acquire feelings of the need to please you.

The following principles are aimed at helping you to teach your child some basics that will lead to her inner conscience and acceptable behavior in later years. One of the most important things for you to help your child with is the development of self-discipline. You teach her how to behave in different situations and model this with your own behavior.

I hear and I forget.
I see and I remember.
I do and I understand.

CHINESE PROVERB

ten principles for your child's behavior

1. follow the golden rule.

Treat other people in a way that you would like to be treated yourself. Your child will seldom give you and others more consideration and politeness than she gets from you. If you are always too busy to help her, or quick to anger, she will not readily help you with simple household tasks or refrain from yelling when it is inappropriate.

2. make sure that behaving well is nicer for her than behaving badly.

Encourage good behavior. It is easy to buy a treat to keep your whining child quiet while shopping. Try giving one to her if she is happily helping you while you shop.

3. try to keep instructions positive.

"Do" usually works better than "don't." Your child prefers activity to inactivity, and being forbidden to do things tends to arouse rebellious feelings. "Bring your snack and eat it here with me" will probably work better than, "Don't eat in the living room."

4. try to keep "don't" for general rules.

"Don't" works well if you know there are behaviors that you generally don't allow, such as, "Don't play with the car locks." It does not work for things like "Don't interrupt while I'm talking," because there are times when you would want her to interrupt, for example, when she needs to go to the toilet. Rules are useful in keeping your small child safe. But if they are too rigid and inflexible, they will not help her learn inner control and inner discipline.

5. try to be clear.

Some instructions sound positive to us, but are vague to your child. For example, "Behave yourself" really means "Don't do anything I wouldn't like." This is not only negative, but also an impossible instruction for her to follow because she can't work out all the things that you might dislike.

6. whenever there is time, tell her your reasons.

Blind obedience will not lead your child to understanding the basic reasons for those vital principles of behavior. If you ask for her obedience, tell her why. For example, if you explain, "Please leave the phone alone because Mommy needs to use it," rather than "Leave the phone alone," she can add this example of behavior into her knowledge of how to behave.

7. try to reserve a sharp "no" for emergencies.

There are many occasions when her safety will depend on instant obedience, with the reasons given later, for example, going near the road. If you reserve the word "no," in that sharp tone, for occasions when you are protecting her from danger, she will come to see it as a protective word.

8. be consistent in your principles but don't worry about exceptions to the rules.

As long as you know the kinds of behavior you think desirable and are consistent about those, it does not matter if you allow exceptions to the rules. The principle is that certain activities are only allowed sometimes. There are always special times and circumstances which may allow for a behavior that you wouldn't allow on a regular basis, such as having treats or staying up late at holiday time.

Even inconsistency between her parents will not confuse your child at this stage if it is honestly discussed with her so that she understands.

9. trust that she means to behave well.

The more your child feels that you are always ready to correct her, the less she will think for herself what she should and shouldn't do. Within the limits of her age and stage, give her increasing responsibility for her own behavior and let her feel that she is trusted.

10. we can all learn from our mistakes.

Your child is watching your behavior and, to some extent, modeling herself on you. She knows that she is not perfect, so admitted imperfections in you make you a better model, not a less respectable one. If you accuse her wrongly or make an honest mistake, you should apologize. She will develop resilience from this and be more likely to learn from her own mistakes.

summing up

In this book we describe emotional and social development separately from other types of development so that we can focus on it in depth. But all development takes place at once, and your baby will not be developing emotionally on one day and physically on another. Every day of your baby's life

is an opportunity to help her grow and to strengthen the bond between you and her. The strong sense of feeling that she is loved and cared for will stay with her long after your role as her hands-on caregiver ends. She needs that strong inner security to face the challenges of life that lie ahead.

recommended reading

- *Your Baby and Child: From Birth to Age Five*, New version, by Penelope Leach, New York: Alfred A. Knopf, 1998.

- *Children First: What our society must do – and is not doing – for our children today*, by Penelope Leach, New York: Alfred A. Knopf, 1994.

- *Growing Together: A Parent's Guide to Baby's First Year*, by Dr. William Sears, La Leche League International, P.O. Box 1209, Franklin Park, Illinois, 60131-8209 U.S.A., 1998.

- *The Baby Book: Everything You Need to Know about Your Baby – from Birth to Age Two*, by Dr. William Sears and Martha Sears, R.N., New York: Little Brown and Company, 1993.

- *The Emotional Life of the Toddler*, by Alicia F. Lieberman, Ph.D., New York: The Free Press, 1995.

accreditation

Emotional and Social Development is based on the work
of many parent educators, most notably Penolope Leach, Ph.D.,
Dr. William Sears and Martha Sears, R.N. and Otto Weininger, Ph.D.

Editors: Dali Castro and Carol Lawlor

Designers: The Adlib Group and Beth Gorbet

Look for these Parent**Smart** Books
at leading bookstores and other retail outlets

Joyful and Confident Parenting

This book is essential reading for every new parent. Here is the information and step-by-step advice parents need from the day their new baby joins the family.

Joyful and Confident Parenting addresses the issue of baby bonding with mom and dad as well as others in the extended family, including other caregivers. Readers will learn the steps to help build solid parent-child relationships that will last a lifetime.

The book examines how each member of the family's parenting team can play a meaningful role in the new baby's development. The chapter entitled *Taking Stock* encourages parents to consider their own personal parenting style, the way they were raised by their parents, and how these factors will affect the way they approach the parenting of their own child.

Topics covered in *Joyful and Confident Parenting* include:

- newborn basics
- your parenting style
- baby-proofing your home
- choosing childcare
- creating a support system
- avoiding some parenting pitfalls
- how to achieve positive parenting
- building a healthy parent-child relationship

This book provides parents with the basics of joyful and confident parenting.

Positive Discipline

Some of the most challenging situations for parents and their child involve dealing with discipline issues. Starting with the basic premise that discipline starts with love, this book looks at changing discipline needs, as children go through early stages of development.

Topics covered in *Positive Discipline* include:
- how discipline techniques can affect a child's self-esteem
- the characteristics of positive discipline
- handling your own emotions and anger
- the trouble with spanking
- discipline versus punishment
- avoiding tantrums
- why you can't spoil with love
- setting appropriate limits

This book provides parents with eight practical strategies they can use to encourage cooperation from their children, and sets out easy-to-follow techniques for handling various discipline issues, including tantrums, defiance and anger. There are sections that provide guidance on dealing with discipline problems when a child is living part-time with separated or divorced parents, and on how parents can better manage their own anger, to the benefit of their children and parenting partners.

Your Baby and Child's
Growth and Development

From the moment of conception, a child's rate of growth and development is determined by a complex combination of genetic and environmental factors. This book helps parents to fully understand the factors affecting their baby's growth and development.

The book is organized into separate sections, each dealing with a particular phase of development, including the first six months and up to preschool. Each section looks at the factors of most concern during the particular period, including weight gain, changes in nutritional requirements, sleep patterns, increased mobility, speech and language development.

Growth and Development provides invaluable guidelines to help parents manage their baby's environment during these first vitally important years.

Topics covered in *Growth and Development* include:

- when to start baby on solid foods
- changing sleep patterns
- physical activities and feelings
- your child in play groups
- what to anticipate at each growth stage
- weight gain
- body awareness
- toddler's self-esteem
- fun and fitness

This book provides parents with an easy-to-follow guide to their baby and child's growth and development.

How Your Baby & Child Learns

Most parents want their child to have a love of learning and to do well in school. Recent research now confirms that there is much that parents can do to provide the care and stimulation which enhances learning in the first few years. *How Your Baby & Child Learns* contains information on numerous subjects, including creating a positive learning environment, a baby's early brain development and dealing with children who have special needs.

This book explores the stages of a baby's intellectual development. It provides information, as well as tips and techniques, on how parents can stimulate their child's interest in reading and how learning music also enhances mathematical abilities.

Topics covered in *How Your Baby & Child Learns* include:

- how the brain is hard-wired
- learning social responsibility
- numbers and quantitative thinking
- learning through friends
- talking to your baby
- stimulating a healthy curiosity
- talking and listening
- learning through play
- learning by pretending
- toddlers and television
- reading to your child
- music and learning

This book gives parents the information they need to enhance their child's learning opportunities.

Medical Emergencies & Childhood Illnesses

This book should have a place of importance in every home with small children. No matter how carefully children are supervised, medical emergencies can happen. And when they do happen, this guide provides easy-to-follow procedures.

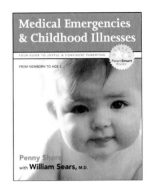

Everything the caregiver needs to know is set out clearly, with instructions on the appropriate course of action. There are three sections in this book: Medical Emergencies, Childhood Illnesses and Your Child's Personal Health Journal. The section on Medical Emergencies covers all of the common situations, including:

- broken or fractured bones
- head and nose injuries
- breathing difficulties
- emergency medical kit
- strains and sprains
- convulsions and seizures
- sunburn
- bites and stings
- choking
- poisoning
- burns
- bleeding
- eye injuries
- shock

A separate section on Childhood Illnesses provides caregivers with an easy-to-understand directory. It includes the symptoms to look for, the action to be taken by the caregiver, as well as an alert on special things to watch for in each particular situation.

The Personal Journal section will provide for an important record of a child's inoculations, illnesses and hospitalizations. It can be used when visiting the family doctor or when traveling.

With children, one thing is certain — illnesses and injuries are inevitable. Having this book conveniently accessible will ensure that information is always available when it is needed.

The International Advisory Council on Parenting

Penny Shore

Created the *ParentSmart Books* and is President of The Parent Kit Corporation. She was Vice President, Product Development for Hume Publishing, and a management consultant with degrees in psychology and gerontology. An expert on the development of home study programs on a variety of topics, Ms. Shore is a parenting educator and an advocate for effective parenting.

Penelope Leach, Ph.D.

Was educated at Cambridge University, London School of Economics and University of London, where she received her Ph.D. in psychology. She is a renowned author of many books, including *Your Baby and Child* and *Your Growing Child*, fellow of the British Psychological Society, past President of the Child Development Society and acknowledged international expert on the effects of parents' different child-rearing styles on children.

William Sears, M.D.

Regarded as one of North America's leading pediatricians, is a medical and parenting consultant to several magazines and organizations, and a frequent guest on television shows. Dr. Sears received his pediatric training at Harvard Medical School's Children's Hospital and Toronto's Hospital for Sick Children. He is the author of many books on parenting, including *The Baby Book* and *The Discipline Book*.

Martha Sears, R.N.

Is a registered pediatric nurse and co-author, with her husband, William Sears, of many books on parenting, including *Parenting the Fussy Baby and the High-Need Child.* In addition to being a regular contributor to several national magazines for parents, she has appeared on more than a hundred television shows and is a popular speaker at parents' organizations across North America.

Otto Weininger, Ph.D.

Served for 15 years as chairman of the Early Childhood Program at the University of Toronto, where he received his Ph.D. in psychology. He is the author of several books including *Time In* and former editor of *The International Journal of Early Childhood Education*. He is a host and frequent guest on radio and television programs around the world, sharing his expertise on children's education, play, learning and relationships.

YOUR PARENTING JOURNAL

Date   **Comments**

YOUR PARENTING JOURNAL

Date   **Comments**

YOUR PARENTING JOURNAL

Date   **Comments**

YOUR PARENTING JOURNAL

Date   **Comments**

YOUR PARENTING JOURNAL

Date   **Comments**

YOUR PARENTING JOURNAL

Date   **Comments**

Date	Comments

YOUR PARENTING JOURNAL

Date   **Comments**

index